Forensic Crime Solvers

BALLISTICS

By Barbara B. Rollins and Michael Dahl

Consultant:
Stephanie Eckerman
Forensic Scientist and Firearms Examiner
Minnesota Bureau of Criminal Apprehension
St. Paul, Minnesota

Capstone
press

Mankato, Minnesota

Edge Books are published by Capstone Press,
151 Good Counsel Drive, P.O. Box 669, Mankato, Minnesota 56002.
www.capstonepress.com

Library of Congress Cataloging-in-Publication Data
Rollins, Barbara B.
　　Ballistics / by Barbara B. Rollins and Michael Dahl.
　　p. cm.—(Edge books. Forensic crime solvers)
　　Summary: Describes the science of ballistics, including the types of weapons and
ammunition used in crimes, clues guns and bullets leave behind, techniques used by
ballistics experts, and how ballistics evidence is used to solve crimes.
　　Includes bibliographical references and index.
　　ISBN 0-7368-2421-9 (hardcover)
　　1. Forensic ballistics—Juvenile literature. 2. Criminal investigation—Juvenile
literature. 3. Evidence, Criminal—Juvenile literature. [1. Ballistics. 2. Forensic sciences.
3. Criminal investigation. 4. Evidence, Criminal.] I. Dahl, Michael. II. Title. III. Edge
books, forensic crime solvers.
HV8077.R65 2004
363.25'62—dc22　　　　　　　　　　　　　　　　　　　　　　　　　2003013032

Editorial Credits

Carrie Braulick, editor; Juliette Peters, designer; Jo Miller, photo researcher

Photo Credits

Capstone Press/Gary Sundermeyer, 4, 6, 7, 8
Corbis, 28; Al Francekevich, 27; Robert Maass, cover; SABA/David Butow, 10
Corel, 1, 12
Folio Inc./Frazier, 24
Getty Images Inc./Don Murray, 26; Hulton Archive, 21, 23; Michael Williams, 18, 22
Index Stock Imagery/Don Stevenson, 15
Ingram Publishing, 29
Photo Researchers Inc./Doug Martin, 20
Unicorn Stock Photos/Tom & Dee Ann McCarthy, 16

2　3　4　5　6　09　08　07　06　05

Table of Contents

CHAPTER 1

Learn about:
- Crime scene investigators
- Collecting firearm evidence
- Using ballistics to solve cases

Weapons Fired!

One late fall evening, three young men sat inside a parked truck. They pulled ski masks over their faces. They then took handguns from their waistbands and ran into a video store.

One of the men demanded money from the clerk. The clerk quietly stepped on an emergency button. The button set off an alarm at a nearby police station.

The police dispatcher checked the alarm's location. She used her radio to call police officers. Two police units driving near the store heard the call. They sped to the scene.

Exchange of Gunfire

The police units met near the store. A gunshot tore through the air as the officers got out of their cars. The video store window shattered. Broken glass spilled onto the sidewalk.

◀ Robbers sometimes wear masks so others cannot identify them.

The robbers and police officers began shooting. One of the robbers fell to the floor. The other two robbers threw down their guns and gave up. The officers ran into the store and put handcuffs on the robbers. The third robber and the store clerk had been shot. Blood flowed from their gunshot wounds. They were already dead when ambulances arrived.

The Investigation

A detective from the police department's internal affairs division arrived. He was there to decide if the police officers had followed department rules. He talked to the officers and people in the neighborhood.

After they arrive at a crime scene, police officers prepare and decide on the best course of action.

CSIs gather bullets and cartridge cases at crime scenes. They place them into evidence bags.

Crime scene investigators (CSIs) arrived to gather evidence. They collected the guns that the robbers and officers had fired. The CSIs also picked up cartridge cases and bullets from the parking lot, sidewalk, and video store floor.

The detective sent the weapons, bullets, and cartridge cases to a lab for testing. The test results would help the detective learn if the officers used their weapons legally. They would also show which gun fired the bullet that killed the store clerk.

Solving the Case

The detective looked at the crime scene photos. The glass from the store's window spilled onto the sidewalk. This meant the robbers had fired their guns at the officers from inside the store. A nearby store owner said the robbers had shot first. Based on this evidence, the detective decided the officers had done nothing illegal.

One week later, the detective received the lab reports. A medical examiner had found the bullet that killed the store clerk. Firearms examiners reported that the bullet came from a .38-caliber gun. Only the dead robber had fired that type of gun. According to this evidence, the robber had killed the clerk.

The detective was satisfied with the information. He finished his report. Firearm evidence from a crime scene had helped him solve another case.

Detectives rely on various reports and many types of evidence to solve a case.

CHAPTER 2

Learn about:

- Types of firearms
- Cartridge cases
- Bullets

Firearms and Ammunition

The study of firearm evidence from crime scenes is called ballistics. It includes the study of firearm types and bullets. It also includes the study of a bullet's path and the damage a bullet causes.

Investigators use firearm evidence to help them solve cases. Some evidence can help them identify the type of gun used in a crime. Other evidence can help investigators understand what happened at a crime scene.

How Firearms Work

All firearms shoot ammunition. Ammunition usually has a cartridge case, a bullet, and an explosive chemical mixture called gunpowder. It also usually includes a mix of chemicals in a pellet called primer. The bullet and gunpowder fit inside the cartridge case. The primer is at the base of the cartridge case.

Firearm evidence can help investigators find
◀ out what happened at a crime scene.

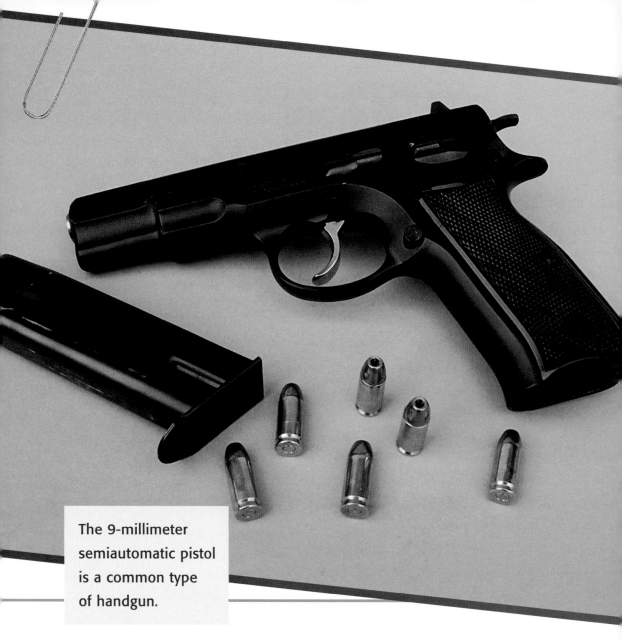

The 9-millimeter semiautomatic pistol is a common type of handgun.

When a gun's trigger is pulled, a spark explodes the chemicals and gunpowder. The blast makes the bullet fly forward. The bullet flies out of the end of the barrel, called the muzzle.

Handguns

Criminals often use handguns to commit crimes. These guns are made to be held and fired with one hand. More than 90 percent of the guns used in U.S. robberies are handguns. They also are used in more than half of all murders in the United States.

Some handguns are revolvers. Revolvers usually hold five to eight cartridge cases. The cases are in a round container called a cylinder. As a revolver fires a bullet, the cylinder turns to line up a new cartridge. The used cartridge case stays in the cylinder until the shooter removes it.

Other handguns are semiautomatic or fully automatic. The cartridge case pops out of these guns after they fire. The gun automatically slides in another cartridge case. Semiautomatics fire a bullet each time the trigger is pulled back. Fully automatic firearms continue to fire bullets as long as the trigger is held back.

Modern handguns have long winding grooves in the barrel. These grooves are called rifling. Rifling makes the bullet spin. A spinning bullet flies farther and straighter toward the target.

Rifles and Shotguns

Rifles are long guns that people fire from the shoulder. Some rifles are semiautomatic. All rifles have rifling in the barrel.

Rifles often hit distant targets more accurately than other guns. For this reason, police snipers use rifles. These officers are trained to accurately hit small targets. They may work in a hostage situation or in another dangerous conflict.

Shotguns are similar to rifles. They are fired from the shoulder. The inside of a shotgun's barrel can be rifled or smooth.

Shotguns can fire shells or slugs. They usually are loaded with shells. Shells contain pellets called shot. The shot spreads out as it leaves the gun's barrel. Slugs are made of solid metal. They are usually more deadly than shot.

Some guards carry shotguns. ➡

Some bullets have a
rounded nose, while others
have a pointed nose.

Types of Bullets

Bullets can be one of several types. Differences between bullets help firearms examiners decide what type of weapon was used in a crime.

A bullet's size matches the inside diameter of the gun's barrel. This measurement is called caliber. For example, a 9-millimeter gun fires a 9-millimeter bullet. Caliber can be measured in millimeters, hundredths of an inch, or thousandths of an inch.

A bullet can be pointed, hollow-pointed, or rounded at the front. A pointed bullet moves quickly through the air. A hollow-pointed bullet sometimes widens when it enters a body. These bullets can cause more damage than other bullets can. A rounded bullet flies slower than a pointed bullet. It sometimes stops at the target instead of going through the target.

Sometimes bullets are wrapped in a thin layer of copper, brass, or steel. These layers are called jackets. Jacketed bullets travel farther than standard bullets.

CHAPTER 3

Learn about:

- Comparison microscopes
- Examining bullets
- Examining cartridge cases

Comparing Bullets and Cartridge Cases

Police bring guns, bullets, cartridge cases, and other evidence to a crime laboratory. Firearms examiners study the evidence at the lab.

Evidence Under a Microscope

A gun's rifling leaves thin streaks called striations on each bullet that travels through the barrel. Each gun makes different striations. Firearms examiners can compare striations on bullets. They can tell if the same gun fired the bullets.

Sometimes examiners can match guns with bullets found at a crime scene. Henry Goddard was one of the first people to trace a bullet back to the gun that fired it. Goddard worked as a police officer in Great Britain during the early 1800s. At this time, gun owners made their own bullets in metal molds. Goddard matched a mark on a bullet to a mark in a mold.

Firearms examiners use computers to study
◄ firearm evidence.

Firearms examiners test fire guns into firing chambers.

Today, firearms examiners load a gun from a crime scene with the same kind of bullet found at the scene. They then shoot, or test fire, the gun into a firing chamber. A firing chamber can be a tank filled with water or padded with cotton.

Examiners compare the fired bullet with a crime scene bullet. They often use a comparison microscope. This device looks like two connected microscopes. It allows examiners to closely view two bullets at the same time. Bullets fired from the same gun will have the same striations.

Firearms examiners sometimes compare cartridge cases from a crime scene. Each gun leaves different marks on the cartridge cases.

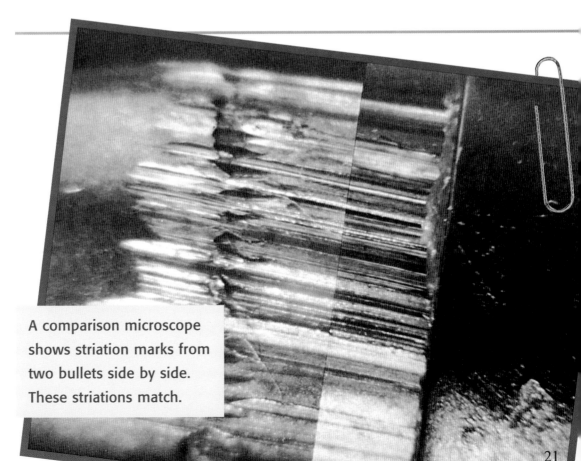

A comparison microscope shows striation marks from two bullets side by side. These striations match.

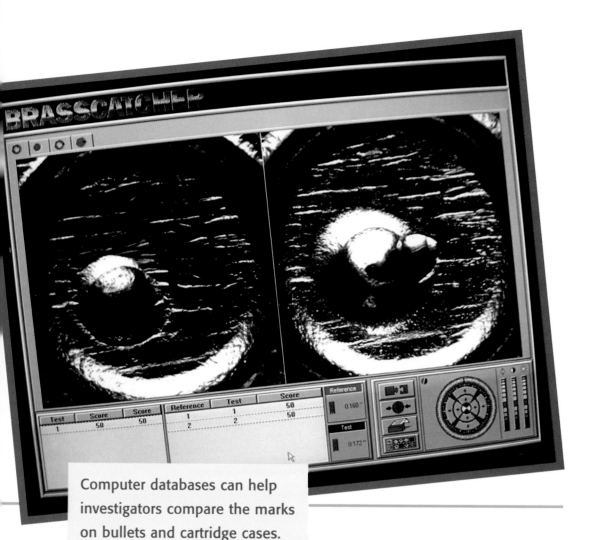

Computer databases can help investigators compare the marks on bullets and cartridge cases.

Computer Databases

Bullets and cartridge cases from crime scenes can show links between crimes. Examiners enter information about the bullets and cartridge cases into a computer database.

The database searches for close matches with bullets and cartridge cases from past crime scenes. A firearms examiner compares the marks on the original bullets or cartridge cases if close matches are found.

Thomas Jackson

In 1863, General Thomas "Stonewall" Jackson was shot on a battlefield during the Civil War (1861–1865). He later died. The bullet was examined. The examiners discovered that it was a 67-caliber ball. The 67-caliber balls were the ammunition Jackson's own Confederate soldiers had used. The Union soldiers they had fought used 58-caliber balls. Jackson had been accidentally shot by one of his own soldiers.

EVIDENCE
POLICE SEAL

Initials
Date
Name

Gunshot Residue Kit
☐ GSR - AA/SEM
82P50002
GSR - AA

Left
Back

Left
Palm

Right
Back

Right
Palm

Other Firearm Evidence

Firearms examiners sometimes do not have guns, bullets, or cartridge cases to compare. Criminals may pick up bullets or cartridge cases. They also may hide or destroy guns. In these cases, firearms examiners study other evidence.

Gunshot Residue

When a gun is fired, the burning gunpowder produces gas and a cloud of particles called gunshot residue (GSR). The GSR sprays out of the gun's barrel. GSR can travel at least 3 feet (1 meter).

GSR can provide investigators with clues. GSR found on an object or person shows that the object or person was nearby when a gun fired. Firearms examiners view the size of GSR patterns on victims' clothing. Large patterns of GSR can mean a shooter fired at close range. Small patterns of GSR can mean the shooter fired from a long distance.

Investigators sometimes check people's
◄ hands for gunshot residue.

Police can use lasers to find a bullet's trajectory.

Trajectory

Bullets sometimes make holes in walls, doors, and other objects. Investigators search for bullet entrance and exit holes. They may be able to determine the bullet's path, or trajectory, by examining the bullet holes. Tracing bullet paths can help investigators learn how a shooting occurred. They may be able to find out the shooter's location when the gun was fired.

Investigators can find a bullet's trajectory in several ways. They may place a rod through the entrance and exit holes. The rod points back to the shooter's location.

Investigators also use laser lights to determine a bullet's trajectory. Investigators point a light at the exit hole and line it up with the entrance hole. The light beam continues to point in the direction from where the shot came.

Backspatter

When a gun fires, it sometimes sucks up air and small objects into the barrel. Firearms examiners call these objects backspatter. Examiners may find tiny bits of clothing, hair, blood, tissue, bone, and other objects in the barrel.

Ballistics and the Courtroom

Firearms examiners sometimes tell about their findings in court. The evidence can help clear or convict suspects of crimes. In 2002, two suspects were arrested for shooting and killing 10 people in the northeastern United States. A rifle found in their car was matched to bullets found at the crime scenes.

Ballistics is a powerful tool for law enforcement officials. Each bullet, cartridge case, or gun can provide investigators with clues. Combined with blood, fingerprint, and other evidence, firearm evidence can help investigators solve even the toughest cases.

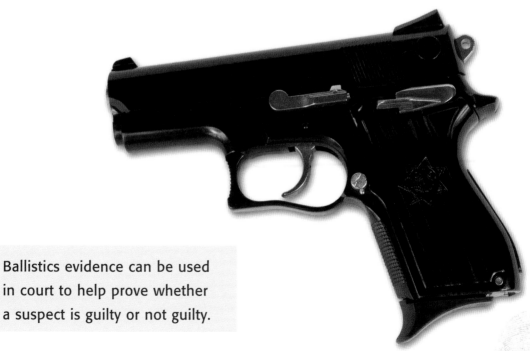

Ballistics evidence can be used in court to help prove whether ◀ a suspect is guilty or not guilty.

Glossary

barrel (BA-ruhl)—the long, tube-shaped metal part of a gun; ammunition travels through a gun's barrel.

caliber (KAL-uh-bur)—the diameter of a gun's barrel

cartridge (KAR-trij)—a container that holds the gunpowder, primer, and ammunition for a gun

diameter (dye-AM-uh-tur)—the length of a straight line through the center of a circle

revolver (rih-VOL-vur)—a type of handgun that usually has five to eight cartridges in a cylinder

rifling (RYE-fling)—grooves in the barrel of a gun that make the bullet travel farther and straighter

shot (SHOT)—lead or steel pellets that can be fired from a shotgun

slug (SLUG)—a solid piece of lead or other metal that can be fired from a shotgun

striation (strye-AYE-shuhn)—a streak on a bullet

trajectory (truh-JEK-tuh-ree)—a bullet's path

Read More

Friedlander, Mark P. Jr., and Terry M. Phillips. *When Objects Talk: Solving a Crime with Science.* Minneapolis: Lerner, 2001.

Meltzer, Milton. *Case Closed: The Real Scoop on Detective Work Life.* New York: Orchard Books, 2001.

Platt, Richard. *Crime Scene: The Ultimate Guide to Forensic Science.* New York: DK Publishing, 2003.

Useful Addresses

Association of Certified Forensic Investigators of Canada
173 Homewood Avenue
Willowdale, ON M2M 1K4
Canada

National Center for Forensic Science
University of Central Florida
P.O. Box 162367
Orlando, FL 32816-2367

Internet Sites

FactHound offers a safe, fun way to find Internet sites related to this book. All of the sites on FactHound have been researched by our staff.

Here's how:

1. Visit *www.facthound.com*
2. Type in this special code **0736824219** for age-appropriate sites. Or enter a search word related to this book for a more general search.
3. Click on the **Fetch It** button.

FactHound will fetch the best sites for you!

Index